Promises and Possibilities:

Dismantling the

School-to- Prison Pipeline

Kelisa JaVon Wing

ISBN: 978-1986423991
Create Space: New York

Books by Kelisa Wing

Conversations

Weeds & Seeds: How to Stay Positive in the Midst of Life's Storms

Promises & Possibilities: Dismantling the School-to-Prison Pipeline

CONTENTS

DEDICATION

Everything I am I owe to God. Not my will, but Your will be done in my life. When others said no, You said Yes. Thank you for being my Lily in the Valley. Thank you Lord.

Thank you to my husband Donald. You sacrifice so much so that I can pour into others, and you unselfishly allow me to share the gifts that God gave me. For that Donald, I am forever grateful. I could not do any of this without your love and support. Thank you for being my husband, my partner, and my best friend. To my children (Donald Jr. , Naima, and Jadon) out of all of my accomplishments, being your mother is the best achievement yet. To my parents (Carolyn (Charles) & Steve (Wanda)) thank you, especially to my mom for your constant love and support. You set a great example of what a woman and a mother should be and how to push through adversity. Thank you to my grandparents: Vincent & Mary Ward. Grandma, you were my first teacher – I am still living off of your life lessons today. To my brother and sister: Shenee & Steven, thank you for always believing in me and being my best friends throughout my life. To my in-laws (Joan – rest in Heaven, Donald, Trina) thank you for your love and acceptance. Thank you to my brothers and sister in-law (Donnisha, Jay, Robert, and Dontay) I love you all. To my spiritual family at Grace Awakening House of Prayer and the I AM ministry (Apostle Lyndon and Pastor Debbie Townsend) thank you for your guidance and teaching me about speaking the truth in love. Special thank you to my Aunt Esther (Necie) Carter, you have always been in my corner. Thank you to my mentors: Ms. Edwina Smith, Ms. Cheryl Lusane, Ms. Debra Alexander, and Dr. Lisa Coleman for the constant support and advice. Thank you to those who contributed to this book: Daniele Massey, Ricardo Castro, Vivett Dukes, Tanya Hill, Dr. Toney McNair, Jr., Megan Gross, Gloria Robertson, Casey Bethel, Cicely Woodard, & the team at Drive Educational Systems, I appreciate your willingness to speak truth to such an important issue.

From my heart to your ears, thank you!

FORWARD:
A PROMISE AND A POSIBILITY

My family has been a pillar in my life. Anyone who has read my last book, *Weeds and Seeds: How to Stay Positive in the Midst of Life's Storms* understands how important my family is to me. My grandmother helped to shape my first thoughts about education and teaching, as she was my Pre-school teacher. Being able to learn from her each day always made me smile and set a strong foundation for my own path to becoming an educator.

I wish my grandmother were here today to see my success and to give me an occasional hug, but the values she instilled in each of us lives on to this day.

My grandmother understood, as an educator, how to meet kids at the point of their needs.

In preschool, she used to have us sing a song every morning:

I am a promise, I am a possibility, I am a promise with a capital 'P'

I am a great big bundle of potentiality

And I am learning to hear God's voice and I am trying to make the right choice

I am a promise to be, anything God wants me to be

What my grandmother was telling us was that we could be

anything and do anything.

Every life has purpose and everyone has potential – this is what

promises and possibilities are all about. We owe our students the

promise to give them as much of an opportunity that we can.

Education is the promise of a better future.

For me, I knew that education could provide me with the promise

of a better tomorrow.

What promise do you provide for our youth on a daily basis?

What possibilities does your presence provide for our future

generation?

Unfortunately, last year, 67% of all suspensions were comprised of

Black and Latino students for wilful defiance. Wilful defiance

infractions are things such as not removing a hat, talking back,

chewing gum, or writing on a desk. Three out of every four

suspensions involve a child of color.

We have a Secretary of Education who refuses to acknowledge the

problem and will not even take the time to visit struggling schools.

She has even rejected the idea, contrary to what the data says, that harsh disciplinary measures have contributed to the school-to-prison pipeline.

What does this say to our children? What promises does this provide to them? Many students who are suspended find themselves referred to the juvenile justice system and 65% of children who have had contact with the juvenile justice system find themselves in the criminal justice system as adults.

Promises and possibilities… are we giving our children a promise or a possibility? Is this happening for ALL of them? For the first time, our children of color are the majority in our classrooms across this nation, as they encompass almost 52% of students in school, yet, this issue impacts them the most.

Doctors take an oath to do no harm; I only wish educators would vow to do the same thing. I truly believe that many of us do not realize or recognize the harm we are doing to our youth of color based on our classroom management and discipline policies, but we are funnelling many of our children from our class to cuffs.

I hope that you will approach this book with an open mind and an open heart. I hope you will understand that ALL of us have a role in dismantling the pipeline, no matter what we look like. The school-to-prison pipeline has been a focus of mine since my senior year in high school, and I find it both a privilege and an honor to be able to share my thoughts, through this book, on how we can dismantle this issue together. Much of what is presented is easy to implement and practical. It is my goal to arm you with the tools to eliminate this issue once and for all.

I hope you will promise to take a close look at yourself, be honest, and determine to identify your biases to change the narrative, shift the statistics, and dismantle the pipeline.

Chapter 1:

Dismantling the Belief Gap:

Metal Detectors and Clear Book bags

Chapter 1

Dismantling the Belief Gap:

Metal Detectors and Clear Book bags

In the neighborhood I went to middle school in, we were treated as juvenile delinquents each day we arrived at our school because we were feared and not loved.

I was not accustomed to being treated this way at my elementary school on the West Side of Toledo. School was a place that I viewed as an environment to learn and grow. I explored, read, wrote, and learned about many people in books from many years ago. I experienced both failures and successes in my learning environment.

Life in that neighborhood was carefree for the most part. We were the only black family in the community and, besides the local bigots, I could go from street to street, place to place, and simply be a kid. Summers were filled with carefree children running, playing, and enjoying their youth with sounds emitting from ice cream trucks. You know the sound, the one that would stop a kid dead in their tracks from whatever activity they were engaged in and yell,

"MOOOOMMMMMM, can I have some money for the ice cream truck!!!!". As we darted for the front door.

Every child in the neighborhood from corner to corner would be there, big Kool aid smiles on our faces, ready to get that cold, sweet, delicious treat from the pied piper of our youth – the ice cream man!

School, at this time, was wrought with its own issues, but namely with the issue of a belief gap in what the small number of students of color could do. The differences between students of color and those who were not was felt in the culture and climate of the school. There was a belief that we were not as capable as our white peers.

This belief gap shapes our education system to this very day. So, what is the belief gap? The belief gap is a gap between our expectations of students of color or low socio-economic backgrounds and those who are from more affluent backgrounds. Some educators have a gap of what they believe those students can do in comparison with others. This gap translates into low student expectations and low rigor in task assignments for our children. The greatest issue with this belief gap is that it leads to a system of children educated by people who do not believe in them and do not wish to invest in their future.

One way to close the belief gap is by strengthening the teacher pipeline for teachers of color. Recruitment and retention is a powerful force to ensuring that students can see themselves reflected in the teachers who are standing in front of them. Whether a child is of color or not, there is a plethora of data that supports that having a diverse teacher is of a benefit to ALL students because of their propensity to believe in the ability of all of their students.

The belief gap lends to the achievement gap, which is a very real issue that we have not quite figured out how to combat since schools were integrated. According to the National Assessment of Educational Progress (NAEP) in 2015, African American students performed 26 percentage points lower than that of Caucasian students in the area of math, and the NAEP test has consistently shown a gap for ethnic groups and students who come from low socio-economic families since the 1970s (Vanneman, et. al., 2015). I strongly believe that two main causes of the achievement gap are the belief gap and discipline systems that keep students out of school and time out of school is time not learning.

After the demise of my family, I had to move away from the place that first introduced to me the issue of the belief gap and found myself in a place that exposed me to the trauma of systemic and systematic criminalization of a generation of youth that would shift the way I view education forever and lead me on a path that would

17

inspire this very book you are reading today. There were several issues with my new school, but namely:

Issue #1: We had a full time police officer who patrolled the halls of our school on a daily basis.

Officer Smith never smiled, ever…

"Good morning Officer Smith" I would smile and say as I walked past him.

I often got no response back, just a head nod as he tried his best to look as hard and uninviting as he possibly could. I viewed school as less of a place to learn and more of an institution where I was to be controlled. A police officer juxtaposed with Edgar Allen Poe and algebra just did not seem to fit together.

Issue #2 Teacher Quality was lacking

One of the first things I noticed in my new school was that the quality of my teachers was not good. Although my previous school had its issues, I truly could feel that the teachers in that school WANTED to be there. The teachers in my new school certainly did not. We could feel this through the way they spoke to us, and the way they acted around us.

Ms. Smith, my Science teacher, was one such educator. Her breath reeked of alcohol, eyes were blood shot red, and she simply existed. I cannot remember anything meaningful occurring in Ms. Smith's class at all besides an abundance of worksheets that I do not quite remember being graded - ever!

There were many other teacher issues, but we will get into that later.

Issue #3 We were made to walk through a metal detector each day and were required to carry a clear book bag in order to enter the building.

When we first registered for school, the registrar handed my stepmother a school list.

Clear bags must be carried at all times.

I thought, *wait...what!?*

As a young lady going through changes in my body, I was mortified. There was no privacy and no sense of discretion for us

19

at our school much like prisoners in jail who are stripped of their rights. However, we were not prisoners, we were students. Parents never questioned this treatment because, to them, this was normal, as this was how they were treated in their inner city schools.

After a while, I forgot what "normal" was.

Each day I passed through the metal detector was another day in which I became desensitized to what this daily process was doing to me and to others.

It wasn't until I watched my friend Tyler being handcuffed in school for talking back to the teacher that I realized something was seriously wrong with the system.

I thought back to my old school, the one where I could walk right through the front door, the one where I had books, the one that was predominantly white, and I realized that the system is set up to ensure that there are no promises and no possibilities for those who live in the hood.

For years and years, people have walked through those machines and have been subjected to systemic oppression by those who should be ensuring that they can have the same access as every other child.

So why this book? Why can I not let this go after many years of being an adult and out of that school system?

Because there are still many children who are criminalized each day in schools across the United States. Because maybe the trauma I and others experienced can convince you that the school-to-prison pipeline is real and needs to be eradicated. Maybe you can believe after reading this book that every child, everywhere, everyday needs to be believed in. Finally, I have to speak truth to something that impacts 67% of students of color each year who find themselves suspended three times more than that of students who are white.

Metal detectors and clear book bags were implemented for every inner city school in our school system because the system "believed" that this was the only way students who looked like me and lived in my neighborhood could be educated.

Through the next few chapters, I want to challenge you question your beliefs, to be honest, and to be willing to question systems

and processes that disenfranchise underserved populations of

people.

Chapter Two:

Dismantling the System

Chapter Two:

Dismantling the System

"Injustice anywhere is a threat to justice everywhere"

– Martin Luther King, Jr.

Schools lost a sense of innocence in 1999.

Driving to school one spring morning, I can remember the

breaking news as if it were yesterday; two students went into their

high school in Colorado and killed 13 innocent people and

wounded many others. Up until then, I had never heard of such a

thing happening in a school. This incident created a need to protect

students by treating every offense as an extreme transgression.

Harsh discipline systems have unfortunately contributed to the

school-to-prison pipeline. Many educators, especially in my school

experience, resorted to sending students to the office for minor infractions that should have been addressed within the classroom environment. Zero-tolerance policies have made it easy to eliminate or get rid of students who were perceived as problems. Rather than training educators on how to handle conflict within the classroom, schools created zero-tolerance policies and assigned resource officers to schools to deal with their behavior. My question has always been, why did we relinquish our control? When did we begin to see our students as criminals?

I did not always have a good handle on classroom management, especially when it came to Tammy and Eric, who could not stand one another. No matter how many times I made them move their seats, they always found a way to argue with one another and make chiding remarks whenever one of them would speak in class. I was teaching 11th grade English, and I never really considered how to best manage my classroom and my students. One day, Eric was being increasingly nasty towards Tammy.

"Stop it you two," I pleaded.

As I turned my back to continue writing on the board, Tammy was out of her chair and waling on Eric. I could not believe what was happening. I ran towards them both and moved Tammy away from Eric. Right then, the bell rang. I sent Eric to the nurse's office to ensure that he was okay, but instead of sending Tammy to the Principal's office, I kept her in my room to talk with her. I knew that if I sent Tammy to the office, she would be suspended for a mandatory 10 days under our zero-tolerance policy.

 As a novice teacher, I was not fully aware of what to do, but I knew that I could not do that. Under our zero-tolerance policy guidelines, if a student was suspended for 10 days, consecutive or cumulative, we automatically had to have a manifestation meeting in which we would determine whether or not they should be expelled. I could not honestly say that I had done all that I could do to avoid this situation; therefore, I could not send Tammy to be suspended for one mistake.

As I spoke with her, I found out that she had a lot of other issues going on in her life; her parents were getting divorced, she was being picked on by several other students, and she was very depressed. I referred her to the school counselor instead. As for Eric, I spoke with him as well and mediated between him and

Tammy during my planning period – Eric also had his own issues going on that he was able to resolve through this mediation.

From that day forward, I implemented a rule in my classroom management plan that no student could get out of their chair without permission. If I would have exercised this rule previously, Tammy would not have been out of her chair to hit Eric in the first place. I am proud to say that I have never had a fight in my class since this incident.

There were three specific actions that I took during this situation that we will address in detail:

1. I adjusted my classroom management plan.
2. I dealt with the students using a graduated discipline system.
3. I empowered the students by using conflict mediation.

Take Back Control

The classroom environment is your domain, and you have the power to create an environment that encourages learning.

First, begin the school year with a firm classroom management plan. A key consideration when designing a classroom management plan is to determine what you believe in prior to starting the design of your plan.

A few questions to consider: What is important to you? Why did you decide to become an educator? Do you believe that every child can succeed? What can you do to ensure that they are successful in your classroom?

1. _____

2. _____

3. _____

Once you have determined the plan, it is a must that the plan is shared with students and parents on the first day of school.

The two rules that I used to guide all the rest in my classroom were:

1. No one can stop the teacher from teaching

2. No one can stop each other from learning

Students understood that these two very simple rules covered just about anything that could take place in the classroom; however, a powerful practice is to allow students to have a voice and choice about what else they wanted to include in that management plan. Asking them how they learn best, what types of things they want to learn about, and what you can do for them are powerful ways to include them in the process while also showing them that they are respected.

It is our job to keep students safe within our rooms and to keep issues that we can control at our level. I also used my classroom management plan as a way to build a sense of community in my classroom. I emphasized the fact that in my classroom, we were a family, so there would be no bullying and no disrespecting each other for any reason. As soon as I saw this or heard this, I called out the behavior and reminded my students that this was not tolerated in my classroom. You have this power as well – you simply have to use it.

So in what ways can you use classroom management to deconstruct the pipeline?

1. **Use your power for good** – see the plan as a way to not just be reactive, but to be proactive. What skills can you teach students through the use of your management plan? How can you extend this to their daily living when they are not in your classroom? See this as a way to help them beyond your four walls.

2. **Show them that they can trust people of authority** – We should always seek to show students that we have their best interest at heart. Through the classroom management plan, we can earn the trust of our students while also showing them that we care. Students want and need discipline, but they also want respect as well.

3. **Involve parents** – I often communicate with my parents to see how we can extend skills to their community. Let your parents know what skills you are working on weekly. Inform them of the management plan so that they can support you.

We have to build a community of support for students. It is not enough to simply teach students math, science, and English, but we must teach students skills to survive in this world. Skills that will last them a lifetime and give them hope and a future.

Graduated Discipline Systems

Under zero-tolerance policies, students have been unjustly and harshly disciplined. One such case involved a student, Andrew Mikel, who was expelled for a year and given a criminal record for shooting spit-balls at other students. The school district claimed that the spit-balls violated the zero tolerance for weapons policy (Supreme Court, 2012). This student was charged in the judicial system with the crime of 'violent criminal conduct' and the spitballs were classified as a weapon. Mikel's family applied to have their case heard by the Supreme Court, yet they were unsuccessful, as the high court refused to hear the case in 2012 (2012).

This is yet another indication of the contribution that discipline systems play in the school-to-prison pipeline. If a child is not in school, they are not learning. The discipline systems must be revised to ensure equitable treatment for every child in our schools.

The idea of a graduated discipline system is not new, but

necessary. In a graduated discipline system, students are punished based on repeated offenses.

For example, in my classroom management plan, the following graduated discipline system is as follows:

1. The first steps for disciplinary action is for me to conference with the student and/or give them a warning.
2. The next step would be for me to inform their parent or to have a conference with the parent.
3. If those steps did not work, then I would refer the child to the office; however, a graduated discipline system in the office would look similar to this process as well.

It is important to note however, that serious infractions will likely need to be addressed at a higher level, especially when it comes to safety.

By having a graduated discipline system, students are given a chance to correct their behavior without being instantly suspended as they would with a zero tolerance policy. A graduated discipline system also allows for an opportunity, through counseling, to find out what is at the root of the behavior a child may be displaying.

Graduated discipline systems allow schools to consider the student, past behavior, and mitigating circumstances. Just like education is not a one-size fits all situation, discipline is not one size fits all either.

Powerful practices to consider when changing discipline systems:

1. **Have a team in place** – Consider having a team that consists not only of the school administrators, but also with the school counselor, a team of teachers, and students who can assist when other issues are discovered. Being proactive and creating a community of support for students can prove to be very effective for students' futures.

Beyond simply having a team in place at the school level, consider having a District team in place to look at the current discipline plan across the system. Many studies have been conducted about zero tolerance policies and discipline systems on a national level. Studies ranging from *Zero Tolerance: Unfair with Little Recourse*, which sought to find an answer to if students' civil liberties were violated (Black, 2004), to *Zero Tolerance and the Paradox of Fairness: Viewpoints from the Classroom*, which asked pre-service

33

and in service teachers what they identified as 'fair' (Fries &
DeMitchell, 2007), and *Are Zero Tolerance Policies Effective in
the Schools*, which studied the affect that zero tolerance policies
have on education and the justice system as well as on adolescent
development (American Psychological Association Zero Tolerance
Task Force, 2008). One of the findings in the aforementioned
studies concluded that violence in schools has not increased, which
seems to give the assumption that zero tolerance policies are not
the answer to disciplinary issues (2008). The focus of this team
should be to explore whether or not their schools are safer as a
result of their discipline policy. The research could identify
schools' disciplinary issues prior to the adoption of the current
discipline policy and after them, and, finally, the result of the
policy on the students. The team could also seek to determine
whether or not their current discipline policy has contributed to the
achievement gap. Ultimately, the team should seek to determine
alternatives to the discipline policy. The team should also look for
trends in discipline systems in an effort to ensure equity, not just in
education, but also in discipline. Statistically, by the time students
are in 4th grade, the prison system is already predicting who will be

in the penal system based on the reading levels of our students. Knowing this is powerful, in that literacy can be a powerful tool to dismantling the pipeline as well. The team should look to dig deep into these issues that lend to the pipeline.

2. **Communicate the plan**: Teachers, parents, and students should all be aware of the graduated system of discipline. The consistent message with this type of discipline system is that schools desire to take back their discipline system and not have students being punished in the penal system.

The communication should extend to us being honest about the problems that contribute to the pipeline in and of itself and what we plan to do as educators and stakeholders to eliminate those issues. The communication also needs to be two-way with our parents, community members, and stakeholders.

A few years ago, I had an opportunity to partner with my local Youth Detention Center. I worked with the Director to find out what some of the students had done to be in the center. 75% of the youth who were there got in trouble at school. We started to look at those behaviors that contributed to their attendance in the program and then worked with School Resource Officers as well as administrators to see what types of preventative services they might explore offering students before they get in trouble so we can be proactive with our youth as opposed to reactive. The school-to-prison pipeline is a systemic problem that will require a system to dismantle, but we must have communication in order to do so.

3. **Use the discipline system to correct and replace** – Not only should a discipline system correct students' behaviors, but it should also seek to correct the negative actions with positive ones. Two programs that can assist in this effort are Boys Town (www.boystown.org), which teaches students social skills, as well as the Overcoming Obstacles curriculum (www.overcomingobstacles.org), which also gives students the skills to be successful. Later on, we will discuss this in the Chapter titled 'Dismantling our Practices'.

Earn their trust

We have to show our students that they can trust us as people in positions of authority. After many police shootings, I felt it was especially important to discuss authority in class. I invited in our local police department in an effort to allow students to discuss topics they would not necessarily be able to or feel comfortable talking about outside of the classroom. From those sessions, we launched a campaign to give students an opportunity to learn more about police officers and vice versa. The rationale was that not all officers are bad and not all youth are bad – we fear what we do not know. We have to have more opportunities where we can create a culture of trust, especially with our students who are prejudged as criminals and are punished more often. Another opportunity would be to have opportunities for staff and administrators to come in and have speaking opportunities with students much in the way we did in the classroom. Home visits are a powerful way to earn students' trusts. Parent universities, which are evenings in which our parents can come in and learn about what we are doing and how we are preparing their children for life beyond school are also ways to flip "home visits". We have to create partnerships to earn trust – we have to become a community in unity to dismantle the pipeline.

Conflict Mediation

One of the final ways that I helped to empower Tammy and Eric in my earlier example was that I allowed them an opportunity to mediate their differences. One of the best things about conflict mediation is that it affords students the opportunity to handle their problems on their own with the support of a mediator.

Elementary School

In the younger grades, conflict mediation can occur with a team of educators who would serve as mediators for the students. When conflicts arise, students can either request a mediation session or be referred by someone in the school community. Although these students are younger, it is important to guide them in the discovery of their own solutions and plans on how to get along going forward. Conflict mediation is such a powerful skill to have in order to become a successful adult, and a program like this can assist them in this area.

Secondary School

In a secondary setting, teams of students in each grade level can be

trained by adults in the tools to become conflict mediators who can

assist their peers in negotiation before conflicts arise. Educators

can serve by sponsoring the students, conducting meetings, and

providing them additional support throughout the process. Much

like the younger students, secondary students should be

encouraged to come to their own solutions with the guide of a peer

mediator.

Sample Peer Mediation Rubric:
1. Give each student an opportunity to share their side of the story (ensure equitable time with no interruptions).
2. After both sides have shared their issues, ask them:
a. What can be done to go forward without any conflict?
b. What can we agree on together?
c. What will we do if a conflict arises again?
3. Each student should be given time to answer, without interruption, each of these questions.
4. Students will sign a mediation agreement, agreeing to the terms they agreed upon during their mediation session.

A conflict mediation program will take time to cultivate; however,

the benefits of creating such a program outweigh the time and effort that the development will take.

Concluding Thoughts

Changing the school-to-prison pipeline begins by changing the way we discipline students. Our schools have to stop looking like prison institutions and begin to be the social change systems that they should be. Students have to know that the education system is a system that can change their current situation into whatever dream they want it to be.

Discipline at the lowest level begins with the individual teacher and the environment we set. The next step, as well as a key component of a classroom management plan is a graduated discipline program, and throughout the process, we have to give students the tools to self-discipline through various means such as through conflict mediation.

While all these efforts are necessary steps to deconstructing the pipeline, they will not change anything unless we are willing to face the reality that some of us have not set high expectations for our students based on our inherent biases. Unfortunately, there are some educators who believe that there is no hope for some of our students. In the next chapter, we will explore how we can examine those biases that sentence our students to bleak futures.

Chapter 3:

Dismantling Your Bias

Chapter 3:

Dismantling Your Bias

Think back as far as you can to your first years in school. Push your mind as far back in your memories as you can. Where are you? What grade are you in? Can you smell chalk? Do you see projectors? Transparency papers? Desks lined in neat rows? Are your teachers direct instructors? Did you ever feel different or see yourself as being different during this time? When do you first recall that feeling?

"Can I lick your cheek?"

This was when I first felt that difference. It was in the first grade when Emily asked me this off the wall question. She must have seen from the look on my face that I was baffled.

"I want to see if you taste like chocolate." she said very casually.

This was when I realized that I was different, and that others viewed me differently.

Without warning, Emily leaned over, whipped out her tongue, and glided it across my cheek.

"You sure don't taste like chocolate." She said as she skipped away towards the swings on the playground, ponytails bouncing in the wind.

In this innocent exchange, Emily recognized our differences, saw them, and acknowledged them in the most innocent way.

I.   If we claim not to see race, we might be biased:

There are some people who say, " I don't see color", as if this is a badge of honor; however, if you claim not to see race, that is a serious issue. I understand that many times, when people say this phrase, they believe that it is a good thing to not see the differences that exist from person to person, but it is quite the contrary.

1. It is inconsiderate to not "see".

I had a student several years ago who had Spina bifida, a birth defect that causes a baby's spinal cord not to develop properly. Prior to her arrival at the school, we all were very ignorant to this defect and its effect on people.

Imagine if I would have made a statement to her parent like *I don't see Spina Bifida,* and then chose to ignore the fact that she had to deal with this defect every day. I would not be valuing or considering how she felt and what she went through. Valerie had to use a wheelchair and use a tube in order to use the bathroom, so I needed to know how those things impacted her on a daily basis. I asked Valerie questions and learned much as I could about her condition. I also allowed her to use her voice with the other students to raise their awareness.

I was honored to have Valerie in my class that year. Her differences allowed every child in my class to grow and to experience how this impacted her. They learned empathy and compassion through that experience. We were better because we did not choose to be inconsiderate and not *see* Valerie.

While race is certainly not a defect, or a condition (please do not miss the point of my analogy) it does play a part in who we are every day, and if we *choose* not to see it, because make no mistake, it is a choice, we devalue others and are not considerate of them.

2. It underscores our bias when we do not see differences

By saying, *I don't see race*, we are really saying, *I don't see you.* We have not earned the right to say that we do not see race or differences in people, especially in a job as complex as being an educator.

Educators are taught to get to know their students. One of the first things an early childhood educator is expected to do is to conduct an in home visit prior to the first day of school for Pre-K and Kindergarten students. We know that we must absolutely build a relationship with our students in order to effectively teach them. Through getting to know them, we must get to know every aspect of our students and learn what makes them who they are and we must see them – all of them.

Reflections from the Field:

To consciously prepare myself to be culturally appropriate, I've spent a lot of time reading, trying to listen more actively to my students and their parents, and providing opportunities for students to share their cultures with me and our class. Before I ever became a teacher, I read this amazing book, *The Spirit Catches You and Then You Fall Down: A Hmong Child, Her American Doctors, and the Collision of Two Cultures*, by Anne Fadiman. This book really help me reflect on my perspectives on what is "traditional" or "appropriate" and how important it is to really listen to my student's families. For the past five years, in addition to my students ethnic and religious cultures, I've also been seeking to understand more about disability culture, so I can better support my students with autism. I've shared resources, such as books or documentaries, with my students and families. Instead of tip-toeing around conversations about disability, my high school students and I have embarked on a journey of discovery, learning how to relate to another's experience and learn from it, and embrace who we are.

Recently, a parent texted me asking if we had been talking about autism in class, as her student, who is nonverbal, had woken up that morning and typed on his iPad, "autism", "cool kid." When discussing educational equity, I think it's important that students with disabilities are included in the conversation. Often when I attend conferences or workshops on equity, the content is driven by the needs of students of color, English language learners, or students from low socioeconomic backgrounds. I wholeheartedly agree that these student groups are students whose needs we are not addressing and need to be addressing in fundamentally different ways. But, I also think in these same conversations, we should also be discussing our students with disabilities. How does disproportionate identification of students of color with learning disabilities occur? What are our biases about students with moderate-severe disabilities and their "ability" to be included in general education classes and environments? How does the requirement for a continuum of special education services leave some students stuck in programs or specialized placements, rather than their neighborhood schools? We must address the educational equity needs of all our students to achieve an educated, engaged, democratic society.

- **Megan Gross, Del Norte High School, Special Education Teacher, 2017 California/ National Finalist Teacher of the Year**

II. If we do not seek to include Culturally Responsive Teaching (CRT) in our instructional strategies, we might be biased.

You just completed your lesson plans on a unit on the writing process. You determined your opening activity, created a pre-test to see what students know before you started your lesson, and designed activities to help teach the concepts to your students. You are ready! Or, are you?

Did you determine how you would ensure that the lesson was culturally appropriate? Did you review your pre-test to ensure that it was free from any potentially biased questions? Did you consider your learners' backgrounds when deciding what activities they may connect with? If the answer to any of these questions is no – your lesson is not ready.

Culturally appropriate instruction is a tool that educators can use in their teaching that mimics students' cultural learning tools. It must encompass the following elements:

1. Setting high expectation for all learners

Do you believe, please be honest with yourself, that ALL students can succeed? If you truly do, you have to set high expectations through your lesson tasks. What does this look like in practice? It looks like rubrics that spells out in plain terms what students need to do in order to be successful. It looks like rigor with differentiation through flexible grouping. It sounds like, "I believe in you", and, "You can do it!".

Reflections from the Field:

When I first arrived at my current school 3 years ago, I had 35 students in an 8th grade honors integrated math I class for high school credit. Only 3 of those 35 students were Black. The rest were White. In our school where over 40% of the students are Black, I knew that something had to be done about their representation in this class. I talked to my principal about my concern, and he suggested that I start an assessment taskforce. I worked with other teachers from our school to revise the requirements for students who took honors courses. Now instead of just taking the top 35 standardized test scores, students go through an application process. We consider their grades in courses, teacher recommendations, attendance, and answers to essay questions. Students express an interest in taking honors courses by completing the application process. These honors classes are now much more representative of the diversity of our school.

Sometimes in order to address biases as a school, we must change the system so that all children have equitable opportunities.

-    **Cicely Woodard, 2018 Tennessee Teacher of the Year**

Too many times, based on our beliefs about what we think students can do, we see a tendency, especially in schools where we have a lot of students from underserved populations, to see tasks that are not rigorous or even underrepresentation in AP or Honors courses. What this says is, "I do not believe you can do this" which translates to bias and the belief gap.

List two to three commitments you will make to ensure that you are setting and communicating to your students that you have high expectations for them – think about your students from underserved populations:

1._____

2._____

3._____

2. Positive Perspectives of families of students

The second aspect of being a culturally appropriate educator is to believe that the families of our students are our partners, and to see them as a companion in the education of our students.

Reflections from the Field:

It has been equally important to find solutions and creative ways to engage parent collaboration. In an attempt to bridge the crucial communication needed among parents of poverty and our school, I pioneered a Saturday Outreach program in which a group of teachers meet on a bus in the parking lot of a targeted trailer park and lead parent-teacher conferences, registration for multiple events and, FAFSA completion, while exposing parents to the resources at their disposal throughout the year. In the same fashion we conduct conferences within households in order to overcome the transportation challenges within this community. The response has been overwhelming. Through Saturday Outreach, we also have been able to create a block leader program that creates ownership within the community and has led to the support of our year-round parent organization, Familias Unidas. Familias Unidas is a parent outreach organization that I help coordinate during the school year. This parent organization educates parents and equips them with the tools necessary to become active participants in the education process. Familias Unidas offers seven sessions throughout the school year related to career exploration, college workshops, parenting, and cultural celebration. During our last meeting of this year, we had over 600 people, which came to celebrate their children's achievements and collaboration with the community. In the same fashion I have tried to collaborate with parents and school districts, I have also strived to unite different content areas that have traditionally been unrelated. As a Spanish teacher, the pedagogical approaches to teaching a foreign language are very different than teaching language arts to native speakers. After being introduced to my new role in the Spanish department, I was able to collaborate with the Language Arts Department and collaboratively address the same deficiencies of standards by using two different languages. The traditional educational system would have instructed the Spanish Heritage students in a similar way that foreign language teachers instruct non-native pupils, yet by bringing collaboration into play, it was easy to address the same state standards from two different perspectives.

> **- Ricardo Castro**
>
> **Elk Grove High School, 2017 Illinois Teacher of the Year**

What do you think when you email a parent, and they do not respond right away, or at all for that matter? Do you think they are lazy? Do you believe that they do not care about their child? Do you judge them without seeking to understand them first?

Reflections from the Field:

> In order to become more culturally aware, I participated in a professional development that focused on having courageous conversations regarding stereotypes and biases that all teachers may have about their students. This was powerful because it identified how socio-economic status (not color) can have negative effects on how teacher view students and parents. We also learned about the effects of poverty on students and ways to accommodate them in the classroom. I came away from this getting a better

understanding of how to deal with students and parents who are economically disadvantaged.

- **Tanya Hill, Kate Bond Elementary/TN/ESL Teacher**

Years ago, I did just this when I believed that Patrick's mother did not care about his success. Patrick was a senior in high school who was failing my English class. I did all I could, or so I thought I did.

I was a naïve first year teacher, still wet behind the ears with Similac © on my breath. I thought I knew it all, and yet, I knew nothing. Sure, I cared about Patrick, and every other child in my class, but I had biases and was not culturally responsive to his needs. It is so important to pause here and say just because I am a black woman does not make me immune to the issues I speak about nationally and in this book, but the point is to talk about the issues – name them, address them, and seek to eradicate them. We all owe this to our children – no matter what we may look like.

With Patrick, I tried what I felt was what he needed to be successful in my class – in hindsight, I tried to make Patrick's square peg fit into my triangle approach. I wish I would have found out what he liked. I was cultured, for my school at least. I used Talib Kweli to teach Walt Whitman and had my students study Drake to learn about slant rhyme band compare that to Emily Dickenson. Almost all of my students loved my approach to literacy, but my style was not what Patrick needed. Years later, I learned how to expose my students to many different genres as well as providing them with an interest survey to see how they wanted to learn in my classroom. Unfortunately, I did not give Patrick a voice in my learning environment.

One day, extremely frustrated, I emailed his mother explaining to her what he would not do. Her response:

I have done all that I can do. Patrick is a senior, and there is nothing I can do to make him care about school. I am done.

With a lump in my throat and tears in my eyes, I sat at my desk with no words to write back. I thought *how can she not care about her son?* I never wrote her back – it is one of my biggest regrets of my teaching career. I, in that moment, did not have a positive perspective of his family.

In retrospect, I should have recognized her frustration. She did not know what to do anymore, and all I had done was confirm that for her. I should have had a more positive outlook on her and the rest of Patrick's family.

Patrick dropped out of school a few months later. Out of every success story I have been blessed to be a part of, out of every child who says, "Mrs. Wing, thank you for helping me to achieve my goals", Patrick never leaves my mind or my heart. By having a positive perspective of his family and being more persistent and engaged with his family, I wonder what might have happened.

After my failure with Patrick, I decided that I needed to reach youth before they went to high school and I decided to teach 8th graders.

Positive perspectives of students' families matter, especially for educators who teach students who are at risk for the school-to-prison pipeline. Be careful what you think of our parents, and be cautious of being quick to judge them.

Reflections from the Field

I can recall Mr. Robert Davenport, Sr., my tenth grade Ethnicity teacher creating and leveraging student engagement through various inconspicuous tactics that he would use in our classroom. It was a large high school in Norfolk, VA which was as evenly divided racially as it was numerically. It resembled the community of which blacks were on one side of the building and whites on the other; the lockers of the black students were on the bottom floor, while the lockers of the white students were on the main floor of the school's front entrance. Mr. Davenport, a black male educator was poised and distinguished, while his white co-teacher, Mr. Carter (I don't remember his first name) dressed the typical preppy way you might expect (I mean a little less coordinated), but the two of them effectively reached each of us who were from diverse ethnic, social, economic, and academic backgrounds. I didn't know it at the time, but their teaching strategies of eye contact, not allowing you to avoid answering their questions, or sitting idle in class, would stick with me like the stripes on a zebra's back! Mr.

Davenport and Mr. Carter got to know each of us for who we were as individuals and used this practice to teach us how to learn together despite our apparent differences. Outside of our classroom were the normal societal ills that were still being flushed out during this post-Civil Rights era. Inside of our classroom, we were benefitting from what I strive for in my teaching practice as experiencing culturally responsive teaching. I am so grateful that this model has been where I received my foundation.

Personal biases of educators often get in the way of effective teaching and learning. Recently, my wife and I attended a parent-teacher conference on behalf of our 15 year old son. As we sat around the table with his English, Science, Algebra 1, and PE teachers, we could not help but notice their personal biases starring us in our faces. We observed that they were armed with documentation to defend their profession and position regarding teaching or saving this black child from his apparent peril of academic trauma. I mean, despite the numerous emails that have been made to keep the lines of communication open, there was this false sense of what to expect from our face to face visit. My wife and I conveyed to these educators that getting to know our son would prove to tremendously change the narrative of him within their classroom. We discovered that their biases had contributed to his desire not to engage with them in teaching and learning. It was also determined we, his parents, were emphatic about our son not becoming a statistic and that success was not only in his future but in his present. We agreed, in the end, that a more established relationship would reveal some very interesting and positive things and that both our son and his teachers would anchor their engagement through offering opportunities for openness and more intentional communication. That there would be discussions that would not be centered on the negative but positive accomplishments. As an educator, a great amount of my time is spent engaging with my students where they are emotionally, socially, and psychologically before I can actually be effective in teaching them.

-    **Dr. Toney McNair, Jr.**
2017 Virginia State Teacher of the Year

Take a moment and think about how you strengthen your perspectives of your students families? What are some actionable steps you can take to do a better job in this area? If you are already doing a great job in this area, how can you assist a colleague with this? *write down 2-3 ideas.

1. _____

2. _____

3. _____

3. Reshape the Curriculum

We all must teach to the standards, and with the standards come the curriculum; however, as an educator, you have the power to reshape the curriculum through your instructional strategies. By thinking about how you can take a lesson and make it culturally relevant for students as well as give it a real-world connection, you can reshape the curriculum.

When you teach students problem solving strategies through project-based learning (PBL), you have reshaped the curriculum, and when you use a lesson to teach students about social justice, you, my friend, have reshaped the curriculum.

Last school year, my students needed to learn about how to design charts and place data on them. There were many ways we could have accomplished this task; however, I used this opportunity to have my students research immigration of various groups of people to the United States. After they researched these trends, they had to create a chart and graph their findings. We did research about Ellis Island, and the students strengthened their understanding that this nation was built on immigration. There are many other ways to reshape the curriculum. One of the most profound ways as well is to expose your students to multiple perspectives through education. Teach them about people who are not commonly studied. Authors like Ta-Nehisi Coates, Esmeralda Santiago, Mildred Taylor, Walter Mosley, and many others who allow students to learn about social justice and varied backgrounds are available through the National Network of State Teachers of the Year (NNSTOY) at (http://www.nnstoy.org/wp-content/uploads/2017/08/NNSTOY-Social-Justice-Book-List.pdf). These resources can provide you with a path to ensuring that you have the tools to be more culturally responsive.

Reflections from the Field:

Creating Mirrors and Windows for Students Through Literacy

It was during my teacher prep program 24 years ago that I had one particular professor who made me see that no matter who you are, or the language you speak, we all have some level of privileges and disadvantages.

It was also during this professor's class that I saw a documentary film that made me think about the lack of culturally sensitive curriculum and literature we have in our classrooms. The film was a perfect example of how educators don't realize that some of the classwork they assign to students is inappropriate because some students are limited to the textbook and literature they are provided, and don't have access to other resources and examples.

After seeing the film, I thought, how are students who are limited to only the resources that are provided by teachers and schools, able to have an equitable education and be successful? This was a turning point as an educator. I started seeing what I was blinded to in my own education. I started noticing that our school libraries and core curriculum are inadequate sources for teachers to teach about diversity and empathy. I didn't realize that stories had the potential of creating **_mirrors_** to empower all children. Even more amazing is seeing how they create **_windows_** for students to see that all children are as unique, beautiful and capable as them. As educators, we need to remember, that if we truly want a diverse nation, then we shouldn't categorize the people who live in it. What matters is that there are so many cultures and people in our world. All our students need to learn about and learn to appreciate this in order see a change in society.

But unfortunately, 24 years later, I still see an issue with our school libraries and core language arts curriculum. I still see that the majority of our books are not as inclusive as they need to be. Today, it is up to educators and school districts to demand publishers think about providing quality, diverse literature that can help teach about diversity and empathy in schools. So as the 2017

Oregon State Teacher of the Year, I have had the opportunity to talk and teach about diversity and empathy through literacy. It is important for all teachers to look at what they are reading to their students and ask themselves these questions: Am I including stories that create *mirrors* and *windows* for all students? Am I reading either stories about real characters that reflect my student population or am I unintentionally promoting stereotypes? Or, am I reading books throughout the year to teach about diversity?

As educators, it is our responsibility to show our students that all people have stories of adventures, hopes, dreams and successes. It's our job to create the *mirrors* that students can see themselves in, as well as create the *windows* for others to see beyond themselves and see the accomplishments of others different than themselves! So, next time you read a book to your students, see who is missing and create an inclusive pathway for all!

- Gloria Pereyra-Robertson, 2017 Oregon Teacher of the Year

4. Culturally Sensitive

A compliment I have heard given to students of color from people who are not of color (and even as recent as three weeks ago about myself) is *You speak well.*

While this may seem like a "compliment", it certainly is not. The first issue with this statement is that it insinuates that people of color are not supposed to speak well. This is another example of the belief gap that we tend to have for students of color. Why should it come as a surprise that someone speaks proper English? It is not something I have ever heard said about a person who was not of color. When we give this "compliment" to students of color, what we are really saying is that I do not have a high expectation that you can do the very thing that I naturally believe everyone else can do – speak.

Are there things that your students of color have done that you may have perceived one way, but maybe you may have misjudged their actions based on cultural insensitivity? Only by making a concerted effort to be a more culturally relevant educator can we ensure that cultural insensitivity does not happen in our schools.

67

What are some other cultural traditions that you know about that may not be well known to others? In what ways can you share that information with your colleagues to raise their awareness?

_____

_____

III. If you have not examined your bias, you might be biased.

Do you have any biases? Please, as Jay-Z so eloquently reminds us, take a "pregnant pause" here before you respond. Have you ever really thought about this before?

I must confess to you that prior to moving to the inner city as an adolescent, I had biases against people who lived in those neighborhoods. I am sure that sounds crazy to you, but it is my truth. Living in an affluent neighborhood early in my life, I was sheltered. I never heard about gangs until I lived in the inner city and found myself surrounded by gang activity.

Much of what I saw on television and the news had conditioned me to fear my own people, but after being surrounded by the very people that society said should be feared and criminalized, I learned more about myself, and, the people I once feared, became my people. At the same time, based on the situation, I became feared by society as well. This is the worst part of the school-to-prison pipeline and the abuse of power when it comes to discipline systems within our schools – our children are being criminalized and educators are conditioned to think they have to fear these children and treat them like criminals.

Through my experience of facing my biases head on, I learned that I was wrong.

My 8th grade Math teacher, Ms. Jones, was truly biased against her students, although I am sure she never really believed this to be true. She thought that none of us were going to amount to much of anything, so she never invested the time in us to even teach us. Because of her resistance to, as she put it, "Waste time on us", I struggled in Math for years, even in College all based on one year with a biased teacher who did not believe in us.

Has your bias hindered you from reaching every child in your classroom? Have you ever truly identified your implicit biases?

Let's be real with each other...

Reflections from the Field:

One quiet weeknight in my house I was cooking dinner as I noticed my husband talking to our teenage daughter about the events occurring in our country. Recently, several shootings occurred where a white police officer shot a black male and the amount of debate around the shootings was creating a divide among white and black people. My mixed race daughter was asking her black father what was going on and why this was happening? I am the white mother of two brown girls. In that moment, my whiteness shouted at me. My thoughts screamed, "Do my girls see me as more than their mother? Do they see me as an ally or an enemy? Do my girls see me as a silent white woman perpetuating the race problem in America?". As a middle-aged white woman, I have made creating an inclusive environment in my classroom a priority. All students, black, brown, and white are respected in my classroom, and I do not tolerate anything less. However, in that moment, due to current events, I knew it was time to reexamine my own bias and be reflective on my own practice as a continuous process. All students are my "kids", so if I am questioning my own biological children's perspective, then I have a duty to do better and be better for all of the kids that walk into my classroom.

Equity, or moving toward equity, is a process that forces teachers to be vulnerable and reflective. It is painful and may create an uncomfortable feeling. Teachers have a duty to role-model inclusive practices - not just because it is politically correct, but because all students have the right to feel valued, understood and loved in their own way - culturally - emotionally - and mentally!!

-   Daniele Massey 2013 State Teacher of the Year

Every day, I make a conscious effort not to allow my past experiences to influence my decisions. Those who have experienced trauma have to ensure that their past hurts do not cause them to misjudge others or hurt others based on their experiences. I cannot assume that all white people are prejudice against me because I dealt with racism in my life. I cannot assume that my children's teachers are going to not believe in them because that was my experience. I have to go in with a belief that people are good and will do good, but that takes a level of faith and a effort on my part – a conscious effort – every day.

Do you do this? What measures will you take to identify your biases going forward? Remember, you can only address what you will identify and admit to be an issue.

In this chapter, we have covered a lot of ground, from acknowledging our differences, to culturally appropriate teaching, to identifying biases, we have truly identified ways that we can ensure educational equity in our classrooms.

Through these measures, the school-to-prison pipeline can be dismantled. If you can connect to your students in these ways and choose to use discipline in a manner that restores students we can deconstruct the pipeline.

What from this chapter will you commit to doing? How can you spread awareness to your colleagues?

Things I will commit to:

_____

_____

_____

_____

Chapter 4

Dismantling the Narrative

Chapter 4:

Dismantling the Narrative

"The time is always right, to do what's right." –

Martin Luther King, Jr.

In the Spring of 2017, I nervously waited for the guard at the Muscogee County Juvenile Detention Center to search me and take my keys. I had just come back from my car for the second time because I was not aware that I was not supposed to have a cell phone on my first attempt at entering, and the second time, I did not know that I needed a second form of I.D – the struggle was real!

It was a hot Georgia day, and sweat was forming in the corners of my forehead.

"Come forward ma'am." The guard said as she waved her wand over my body.

I had been going through this back and forth process for two months trying to be able to speak to the youth who were in the juvenile detention center. It was not easy, but one thing I have committed to do in my life is to do hard things.

During my first visit, I felt my heart beating out of my chest as I walked through a fence lined with barb wire. As the door slammed shut, I jumped, realizing that I was locked up and unable to get out. I had a moment where I could not wait to leave, and in that moment, I thought about all of the youth who were in the facility and were unable to do what I would be doing as soon as I finished speaking with them - depart.

It took a lot of prior planning and background checks to be able to come in and speak to the youth, but I knew that no matter how difficult the process was, I needed to be there.

After four visits, the day had finally come to speak with the youth. There were 70 teens in the center and almost everyone one of them started their connection to the center through an infraction that they had at their school. Nervously, I waited for the teens to come in to the cafeteria.

Janelle* was there before anyone arrived.

"You *wanted* to come here today?" She said with a confused look on her face.

"Of course I did."

"Why?" She snapped back.

I explained to Janelle that I wanted to try to help them to see that there was another way than the path that they were on.

"People don't come and speak to us." She said with a sincere look on her face.

"Well, I am here because I want to be here, because I believe in you."

As the students entered in the room, the first thing I noticed was that there were only 12 girls out of the group of 70. The second thing that I noticed was that there were only two white children amongst the group, and there were eight Latino children. The other 60 youth in the detention center were African American. I told the students about my life and how I grew up without a lot, much like them, but that I realized that the very fact that I was on this earth showed me that my life was a promise and that I was full of possibility. We spoke about second chances, and the quote by Martin Luther King, Jr. that emphasizes that they have a choice to be something and to begin again at any time.

I have spoken all over the country, from Italy, Germany, California, Michigan, South Carolina, New Jersey and Alabama, but being in that space with the children who many have forgotten provided me with more joy than any speaking engagement could afford me with.

Janelle

At the end of the session Janelle lingered behind. She told me that the first time she got in trouble, it was because she doodled on her desk. Because she *drew* on her desk, she was suspended from school – she was five years old. Janelle was sent to the Principal's office almost every other day in Kindergarten.

"It got to the point where I just stopped caring." She said as she stared off in the distant as though she was trying to remember when she lost her hope.

She explained that she started failing many of her classes because she was not able to keep up with her studies during her time out of school.

Janelle got into a fight in school and got arrested – this was her first time getting in trouble with the law.

From that point on, everything that happened at school caused Janelle to have to go to Juvenile court. Eventually she was placed on probation. Due to something she did outside of school, Janelle was sent to the detention center for nine months. She excitedly told me she was getting out in a few weeks.

She thanked me for coming and told me that she was going to do better with her second chance. Janelle was only 15 years old.

I had to really try hard not to break down as I spoke with Janelle. I found myself wondering where did we go wrong with this young lady? How did we get here? What are we going to do in order to ensure that kids like Janelle do not end up in the system?

Marcus*

Marcus stayed after as well. While it was apparent many of the young men were paying attention to the words I was speaking that day, I noticed that Marcus was especially engaged. Often, I would see him nodding his head in agreement after I would explain an idea or a thought to the group.

"I transfer to County next month when I turn 18." He said after we spoke for a while.

I never asked him what he was there for or why he was being transferred. His story was similar to Janelle's in how he started getting in trouble in school.

"Do you really believe that *I* can still be somebody?" He asked me with trepidation and hope in his voice.

"I KNOW that you can be somebody, and you ARE somebody right now. You don't have to follow the narrative that people have told you Marcus, you can change the story – you can make a new ending."

We spoke for a while about how he could help people with his story. That while I am passionate about helping youth to overcome, him being much younger and speaking his truth could help so many others.

I got ready to leave as the guards told them both that it was time for them to go.

"Come back again and talk to us, please." Janelle said to me before I departed.

"I will." I told her.

****

Marcus and Janelle, in that moment, had hope.

What do we consciously do to ensure that every child we encounter can have hope?

I think about Janelle and Marcus often, and I pray that they both heeded our conversation and changed their narrative.

So, how can we start to change the narrative in our school communities? The first way is to be their advocate.

S.T.A.R

My first year as a middle school teacher, I recognized that the students were really having a lot of struggles. Making the transition from Elementary School to Middle School brought a lot of challenges to these adolescents. The major issues they were faced with were managing conflict, managing time, and making positive choices. I started talking with the administration about the need to create a mentorship program within the school; however,

81

they were not invested in the idea.

That did not stop me. As you try to implement changes, you will be faced with a no and with some adversity, but when you are working to make positive changes, you have to persevere in the face of difficulty.

So, even though I faced rejection on the level of the whole school, I started my idea to mentor students within my classroom, and I began by having my students set quarterly goals:

Sample Student Goal Setting Sheet:

Student Name_____ Date _____

I. Student Agreement

I, _____, will do everything I can to reach my goal by the end of the semester. I have met with my teacher sponsor to discuss the goal and plan. I will work with my teacher-mentor routinely to make sure I am on track with my goal and plan.

Goal:1 _____

My goal will be reached by the end of the following semester:

1st 2nd Semester _____ School Year _____

(Circle one)   Student

Signature_____

2nd 9 weeks Follow-up _____ (Date)

Where are you with your goal? How can I help you?

_____

3rd 9 weeks follow up _____ (Date)

Where are you with your goal? How can I help you?

_____

4th 9 weeks follow-up _____ (Date)

Where are you with your goal? How can I help you? What is your

transition plan for next year? How can I help you?

_____

At the end of every week, I made a point to meet with every child in each of my five classes to check in with them to see how they were doing and what they needed in order to feel supported, safe, and successful.

Is this something you intentionally do with your students?

If not, what are one to two ways that can you show students that you care about them beyond the curriculum?

1. _____

2. _____

My mentorship program grew into a grade level program that I called #Squad Up for Education and eventually I developed it into a non-profit organization. I knew that we had to become a team, or a squad, to achieve the goals that we set forth for our students. We saw such success with this program, that I developed it into a school-wide program that allowed us to assign every child an advocate. I called this program S.T.A.R, which stood for stop, teach, affect, and reach:

S.T.A.R. program:

STAR Advocate Program

S.top. T.each. A.ffect. R.each.

Our students are stars; did you know that no two stars are alike? Like stars, our students are different, unique, and individuals. When you are the star – the focus is on you, and this is exactly what our students need – to be the center of attention – to be a star! Our improvement priority is to enhance the formal structure to provide an adult advocate for every student. All students need is a journal that would be housed in the 1st period teacher's classroom. This would be a quick place where a student could share any issues or problems that they are having or anything that they would want to celebrate.

Stop: We will stop for the first ten minutes of 1st period on Friday. During those ten minutes, there would be no announcements or interruptions with the exception of an announcement reminding that today is a STAR day. There would be one star day per week.

Teach: Although we are not teaching content during this time, we are teaching and fostering a relationship with our students during this time and encouraging them to reflect through the activities. A list of potential STAR activities would be provided to every HR teacher to use throughout the year, reminding students that we are their adult advocate.

Affect: To affect a life is to make a difference, which is what we want to do. Many students need an adult advocate to motivate them and remind them that someone is rooting for them and cares for them.

Reach: We want to reach every child where they are. We want to empower them beyond the curriculum and prepare them for life. We can reach them by building, establishing, and advocating for them.

We saw disciplinary issues decrease by 75% as a result of giving children an advocate and an opportunity to be heard. What made this program such a success was the fact that as we implemented it, we gave teachers the activities to do so that they would not have to come up with them on their own or feel like they had to create something in addition to their lesson.

Sample STAR activities:

Potential STAR Activities (suggestions only – you have the autonomy to create your own; however, during the time provided, all 1st period teachers will be expected to be doing a S.T.A.R. activity):

1. Share weekly reflections

2. Two truths and a lie

3. Identify something nice someone did for you over the course of the week

4. Discuss current events

5. Set a personal goal for the week

6. Discuss a conflict you may have had over the course of the week

7. What will you do over the weekend?

8. Pass the ball – when you have the ball you have to share something that is your favorite

9. Tell the students why you decided to teach

10. Tell the students what the word advocate means and why you are their advocate

11. Family time – talk about your family

12. Discuss ways we could uplift one another

13. Pick one person to do something nice for in the upcoming

week

14. Play a board game

15. Have one-on-one talk with students

16. Have students write STAR reflections in a STAR journal

17. Have students write about anything they want in their STAR journal and share it.

18. Discuss ways to solve conflicts

19. Discuss ways to prepare for change

20. Talk about their future

21. Share funny a story

22. Talk about yourself when you were their age

23. Discuss, "If you could visit any place in the world, where would it be?"

24. After students do something nice for someone, ask them how they felt about it.

25. Challenge students to have a day of integrity: for one whole day be honest. *Don't lie, cheat, keep all your commitments, don't gossip, etc.

26. After the day of integrity, ask students how they felt afterwards.

27. Talk about some things that the students believe in – what do they value??

28. Make a commitment to make better decisions – have

students write in their STAR journal an area that they struggle with making better decisions in – and have them commit to making better decisions.

29. Have students write about how they are doing with their commitment to make better decisions. What is the hardest part? How can I help you as your advocate?

30. Role play

31. Discuss ways to be a better friend to others – allow students to share their ideas

32. Have open discussion about the day's events.

33. Free talk (like free write) – ask the kids what they want to talk about

34. Talk about how to handle gossip – share experiences amongst the group

35. Talk about the importance of showing respect

36. Talk about why you love teaching

37. Family day – allow students to talk about their family

38. Free write – allow students to write about anything they want in their STAR journal.

Because there were 38 Fridays in the school year, we provided teachers with 38 different activities to choose from. Not only did we see a decrease in students' disciplinary problems, but we also saw an increase in students' empathy levels. Not only were students excited for "STAR" Fridays, but our teachers were excited for it as well. As advocates and mentors to our students, we used the time to talk about various topics such as kindness, empathy, and consideration of others.

How do you think a program such as this could benefit your school?

Write down one to two ideas:

1. _____

2. _____

Our STAR program changed the narrative for many students and it closed the belief gap for many educators. Our teachers discussed how this time that they had with students allowed them to get to know them in ways that they had not been able to do before.

If we want to truly dismantle the school-to-prison pipeline, it is going to take us being intentional and purposeful about what we do and how we do it. Teaching students is a high calling that requires us to go deeper than the curriculum.

It took me three years to get the STAR program going, but I was resolved to do something during that time and not allow a 'no' to stop me from doing what I knew was right for our students. I started with my 95 students because they needed someone to believe in them. I did not have discipline problems in my classroom – ever - because my students knew that in room 134, they mattered and were valued. Eventually others started to see the changes in my students and how students began to change the way they viewed education. The following year my colleagues agreed to adapt the model and we started to do it for our 8th grade students. Once others began to see the progress that we were making on our grade level, my Administrators wanted to know more. I named the program STAR because I believed in the potential of our students and wanted to make them the center of attention. Before we knew it, the entire school was taking part in the STAR program.

Reflections from the Field:

As an adolescent, I clearly remember the devastating effects of being poor and Latino. I saw the world from my local setting and perspective since my parents did not have money and we were never able to travel. My adolescent life was continually driven by survival and relationships, and the present was more important than the future. This worldview is why I placed so much emphasis on romantic relationships and developing my "street credit." I observed that many of my students shared this same worldview as I once did, and it propelled me to find solutions that would transition students to a worldview that was conducive to academic achievement. The solution came in the form of an advisory/cultural curriculum through the student development corporation named Umoja. A handful of my colleagues and I took on the role of implementing this advisory program at our school. This advisory curriculum would influence all 1,800 of our students. Titles within the curriculum included: Connecting to the Right Supports, Staying on Track, Malleable Intelligence, Attendance Predicts Success, Road Map to Success, Healthy Relationships and Family, Personal Choices, Dream College, Intro to Transcript Review, Dating Violence, Power of Manhood and Womanhood, among others. Exposing children of poverty to these basic life lessons created a culture that slowly moved to an academic worldview by using a culturally appropriate approach. Advisory curriculum enabled many students to think about self-governance and self-sufficiency, make decisions based on their future goals, strive for achievement, and see life outside their local settings. I was proud to see the results at the end of that year in which our school increased attendance, reported better test scores, and was removed from a lower level of probation.

Throughout history, many well-meaning people from privileged social classes have controlled the stakes of education without a clear sense on how to approach those within poverty. I believe that I bring to education the much-needed diversity that creates cooperative solutions based on understanding what it means to live in poverty and among a culture that is disenfranchised and misunderstood. Through my experience and knowledge, I strengthen the teaching profession by broadening the role of education to include social reform, creating biculturalism and implementing practical cost effective solutions to education. First of all, the importance of educating students and parents is crucial to creating a model of transformation that comes from within the community. For far too many years, there has been a dependence on someone or something from the outside to come to save people from the tragic environment of poverty. It is my duty to show the teaching profession the incredible potential that lies within disadvantaged communities. It is evident that collaboration and sound pedagogy are needed; yet through teamwork, I have brought the potential of these community members to light throughout my career. In addition, I expose the lack of bicultural training that is needed throughout the education profession. Bicultural training is needed to create pedagogical bridges between social classes and cultural backgrounds. As I have worked with future teachers through the UIC education program, I have been a strong conveyor of being 'bisocial'. 'Bisocial' may not be an actual word, yet I believe it transmits a clear need to address the acquisition of worldviews found in children of poverty and those of middle and upper class families in order to create curriculum that scaffolds character and knowledge without the use of negative judgments. It has been frustrating to observe many teachers degrading and ridiculing students because they are unaware of the consequences that derive from poverty. The lack of being "bisocial" interprets behavior and attitudes from a person's own upbringing and not through sound pedagogical training that leads us to resolve the academic and social issues at hand. This social incompetence among some teachers, in turn, creates discouragement in students and leads them to find an alternative identity of power not belonging to school, ultimately lowering academic and social achievement. As an advocate for our children, I strive to bring the much-needed awareness of this issue through collaborating with my colleagues, school districts and parents.

- **Ricardo Castro, Elk Grove High School, 2017 Illinois Teacher of the Year**

My spiritual leader Bishop (Apostle) Townsend reminds us to use what we got, start where we are, and do what we can.

Sometimes all it takes is for us to reach one child. While our ultimate goal is to dismantle the school-to-prison pipeline, if we can change the narrative for one child, we have made a difference.

Do not look down on what others may view as humble beginnings.

Imagine what would have happened if I stopped at the first 'no'?

What is it that your students need for you to do to dismantle their

barriers to equity? What do your students need to dismantle

society's narrative about them?

What is something that you have wanted to do to change the

narrative for your students? What has hindered you up until this

point? *Jot down your ideas.

_____

_____

_____

_____

Chapter 5:

Dismantling Their Boredom

Chapter 5:

Dismantling Their Boredom

"How is school going?" I inquisitively asked my niece the other day.

"Boring!" She emphatically stated.

I pressed her – *why…*

I think she thought I was upset with her, but I genuinely wanted to know what made school boring to her – a fourth grader.

Statistically, girls of color begin to struggle in the areas of Math and Science in the fourth grade.

She explained to me that she never works in groups or collaborates with other students – I listened, clutching my imaginary pearls. She went on to say they do a lot of worksheets – gasp!

97

My heart sank. Is it any wonder that students begin to act out in class, which causes them to get into trouble, which leads to office referrals, and feeds our children into the school-to-prison pipeline. Much of the way that we can disrupt and dismantle the pipeline happens in the planning and delivery of instruction. You, yes you, as the teacher are the first line of defense to managing classroom disruptions and shifting disciplinary actions from punitive to restorative.

So what to do about boredom?

First, find out what your students like through an interest survey:

Sample Interest Survey:

INTEREST SURVEY   NAME:
1.   What is your favorite activity or subject in school? Why?
2.   What is your least favorite activity or subject in school? Why?
3.   Rate the following topics according to your interests:
Reading
Writing

Math

Science

Drama

Music

Physical Education

Geography

History

Art

4.   What are your favorite games or sports?

5. What are three things you like to do when you have free time (besides seeing friends)?

6.   What clubs, groups, team, or organizations do you belong to?

7. If you were going to start a movie club, what kinds of movies would your club watch?

8. If you were going to start a music club, what kinds of music would your club listen to?

9. If you were going to start a book club, what kinds of books

would your club read?

10. If people were to come to you for information about something you know a lot about, what would the topic be?

11. When you're using the computer, are you usually playing games, doing homework, doing research, visiting web sites, visiting chat rooms, shopping, exchanging e-mail, or some other activity?

12. What else should I know about you?

13.   In school, I prefer to work:

☐ alone ☐ with one other person ☐ in a small group ☐ in a larger group

14.   In school, I learn best:

☐ alone ☐ with one other person ☐ in a small group ☐ in a larger group

Interest Surveys give educators an idea of how their students learn best while also providing a way to personalize students' learning to their needs. Too many times, we want a child to walk into our classroom and fit into our contrived idea about how they should behave and how they should learn, but education is not a one size fits all model.

There are several ways that we can ensure that we are adapting our classrooms in a manner that adjusts to our students' learning needs:

1. **Shaping the Environment**: The classroom environment should be conducive for learning. This not only means that the space should be a learning environment, but also that there are well established norms, and classroom management present for learning to take place. When we shift the curriculum, the use of the classroom environment should be changed as well. The environment should also be one where students feel safe to take risks. Recently I visited my friend Wendy Turner (2017 Delaware Teacher of the Year) at her school in Wilmington, DE. The experience touched my spirit! This teacher absolutely gets it!!! Her students are unafraid to be vulnerable, to take risks, and they trust each other and her. They are truly a family. These students, who are only in the 3rd grade, are making the kinds of connections that will last them a lifetime, and this

is a direct reflection of the classroom environment that Wendy creates.

2. **Planning**: I often say that if you fail to plan you can plan to fail. Changing up the curriculum requires educators to study research-based strategies that will allow students to want to be in the classroom. We have to make a plan and follow it through. We have to plan for the learners and their different needs in order to adjust our teaching to meet them where they are and not the other way around.

3. **Listening and Responding**: It is great to think about students and how we can facilitate active listening and speaking in order to increase their desire to participate. We can use oral and non-verbal cues, and also give students feedback on how to maintain or improve. We should also allow for the conversations to be student-led. I visited a close friend, Ms. Sia Kyriakakos (2017 Maryland Teacher of the Year & 2017 Finalist for National Teacher of the Year), and saw her providing rich opportunities for her high school students to be able to share and receive feedback

from her and other students. She has created an environment for her students in which they are empowered and willing to participate. It was a beautiful sight to see – this is how all of our schools can be, but it must start with us.

Another way to dismantle students' boredom is through giving students a voice and a choice through various ways:

Genius Hour

While this concept is unquestionably not something I created as an educator, it certainly MADE my students want to be in the classroom and catered to their interests. The idea of Genius Hour was inspired by Google's policy that allows employees, who are performing well in their roles, to spend 20 percent of their time working on projects that are aligned with their personal passions. One summer, I decided I wanted to give my students one day out of the week where they only worked on a Genius Hour project. I sought out as much research as I could find about the program, and found a book titled, *The Genius Hour Guidebook: Fostering Passion, Wonder, and Inquiry in the Classroom* (2016).

As the title suggests, my students' wonder, inquiry, and passion were certainly ignited. We began with a Wonder Wall, which simply meant that my students started out with a thought of, "I wonder…" Some students wrote things such as, I wonder how we can spread kindness through our school; I wonder how we can eliminate all wars, or I wonder how much college will cost when I reach the age to go. The possibilities were endless. The students placed their thoughts on a sticky note and we placed them all on our Wonder Wall. When a student was at a loss for what they wanted to do, they were able to go to the Wonder Wall and get an idea. Students looked forward to Genius Hour because it was something THEY were interested in, not something I was telling them to do. I even had a student build a roller coaster that was operable all during Genius Hour time. This time was vital because they were able to focus on their passion, and isn't that one of the purposes of education – to assist students in discovering their passions?

Genius Hour Project Completed by a Student:

Students' final product from Genius Hour had to be presented in a creative and innovative way. I encouraged them to push beyond just standing in front of the classroom and reciting what they did. I was more interested in their research as opposed to the actual finished product – it was more about the journey for them to get to the finished product. Imagine what something like this could do to keep students engaged as well as communicate to students the idea that you are willing to allow them to discover and learn about what they want to learn about. The purpose of education is helping students to find their calling, and Genius Hour allows this to happen.

Bistro Tuesdays

As a way to increase my students' desire to read in a more interactive way, once a week, I would set the classroom up like a coffee shop, with snacks and beverages, and allow students to read books on subjects they found interesting, including those about current events.

Students then had to write a paragraph on what they read and learned ensuring that they predicted what they thought would happen next, and they had to define at least five difficult words. Rather than allowing students to look up words they did not understand using laptops, I encouraged students to use physical copies of the dictionary to promote curiosity and awareness of the use of dictionaries, which I found many students were unable to do. By having students to reflect on their reading in a relaxing environment, I was promoting the idea that literacy mattered.

Whether you know it or not, we have 720 days to get students literate from the time they walk into school. What I mean is that by the 3rd grade, our students begin testing, and prisons take the test data and determine, based on scores in reading, how many prisons they predict that they will need based on those numbers.

720 days – let that sink in – some people profit off of the failure of our children. We must dismantle that through ensuring that literacy is at the forefront of everything we do. I cannot tell you how many parents have said to me, *my kid just doesn't like or want to read.* Well, it cannot be an option. It is as vital to be literate as it is to breathe, eat, and drink. Instill into your children the importance of reading – dismantling the pipeline has to start at home just as much as it must occur at school.

Stop saying no

Schools are no stranger to rules. Rather than creating an environment where students feel like they have to walk on eggshells, try telling students what they can do in your classroom. As long as students take responsibility to clean up after themselves, don't distract others, and get their work done, what is the harm in allowing them to have flexible seating, chew gum, or eat in your classroom? Why can't your students stand up and do their work if that is what would help them? Stop saying no – stop focusing on the negative aspect and make your classroom a positive one – just say 'YES'!

By starting with what they can do, students viewed my class as a place where they could be themselves and get comfortable. They knew this was OUR classroom – this was OUR space, and they were free to feel safe, loved and nurtured in that space.

Rethinking Homework

"Why are you giving homework?" My Principal asked me during my first year of teaching. I was shocked. I thought that was what teachers did – assign homework.

I had a lot of students failing that year – because of homework. That was not fair for them because you never know the traumas and situations in your students' homes or the education level of a parent in the home that can help. So if a student is failing because of homework, you have to fix that. I decided to call my homework "evening enrichment" and made it worth 10 percent of the grade.

How could I fail a child for something they were doing at home? There should be multiple pathways to success in your classroom and one test or one assignment should never be the measure of a pass or fail situation in your classroom. Many times, I would have students who finished the homework, but because they were not always organized, they would forget to turn it in. We have to rethink homework and how we use it.

Build relationships with students:

How often do you just simply come into your classroom and just have a conversation with your students? Not introducing a new lesson, or talking about a standard, or preparing for a statewide test, but simply connecting with them. Asking them, how are you doing today? Did you eat this morning? How can I help you? What do you need? How is your family? Did you sleep well last night? When was the last time you did that? I challenge you to start your day out with your students simply talking with them and engaging with them.

How can you more intentionally connect with students and show them that you care about them beyond the curriculum?

_____

_____

_____

When students are bored, they begin to act out and get into trouble. When we keep them engaged from minute to minute and bell to bell, they do not have time to be distracted, be bored, or be engaged in activities that would get them into trouble. We owe it to our students to give them meaningful activities that reach them where they are and bring them to where we want them to be. I am not asking you to shoot off fireworks in your classroom, or do backflips, but I am asking you to keep your curriculum engaging and to plan activities that are interesting to your students.

I love Shakespeare (don't judge me), but my 12th graders did not, so I had to figure out how to make it connect to them. We began to reenact parts of his plays by using modern language. By doing this, my students could truly understand what Shakespeare was talking about. They started to see all of the elements he was introducing, and, although they did not love him, they were able to learn what they needed from that unit. I had to find an entry point. What is your students' entry point?

Allow them to collaborate

Students need to be able to work in differentiated groups that are determined based on data. Grouping students should maximize their opportunity for success, draw on the skills that they possess, and give them a chance to work together with others.

Collaboration is a tool to help students to become both college and career ready, as they will be expected to be able to work with others in whatever career field they choose to go into.

One fallacy that many educators have is the idea that if students are sitting together, they are working together. True collaboration occurs when students are assigned to a specific role (i.e., Recorder, Group Leader, Artist, Bridge Builder, Diction Detective, etc.) and responsible for creating an assignment that allows them to work together to generate a final product. Students should also be grouped based on data – this is called flexible grouping, which can refer to whole group, small group, and partner groups. This type of grouping should occur multiple times of the day, as this increases student achievement.

Student engagement is a critical element to eliminating the school-to-prison pipeline and it is a direct correlation to our classroom management. All of the strategies mentioned in this chapter will support in increasing student engagement. You have the power to dismantle the pipeline, but you have to change your practices. Changing practices will require a shift in our mindset before it happens within our classroom, but if you are committed to this work, you will make the necessary changes.

Eliminate their boredom and increase their engagement!

Chapter 6:

Dismantling our practices

Chapter 6:

Dismantling Our Practices

In order to accomplish all of the things we have discussed thus far, we must have to completely dismantle our practices in our school system. Although we spoke earlier about becoming more culturally appropriate, we must truly come to an understanding of what that truly means. We have to develop our cultural competency in order to change our practices.

Develop your Cultural Competency

Developing our cultural competency requires for us to have an open mind. We have to allow ourselves to be vulnerable and admit that we have a lot to learn. Having an open mind requires you to be uncomfortable. Recently, I was speaking at a conference about this very topic, and a participant explained that as a white man teaching in a predominantly black school, he was often uncomfortable, but he maintained an open mind and embraced the discomfort. Another participant, an Assistant Principal, stated that his school was comprised of 99% English as a Second Language students, and he was a Black male, but having an open mind showed him that he needed to surround himself with people who could help him to develop the skills that he needs to meet the needs of his students. What is it that you need in order to be more open minded about developing your cultural competency?

One way to develop cultural competency is to be more self-aware as well as aware of others. Becoming self-aware is important in this process:

1. What do you believe in?

2. Do you reflect on your actions?

3. Do you ask other people for feedback?

4. Do you know your strengths and your weaknesses?

Becoming self-aware actually allows you to be more aware of other people and how they see you.

The next step to developing your cultural competency is to become adept in cross-cultural skills. Last summer, I went to Finland. Prior to going there, I started doing research on the people, the culture, and the country of Finland. I did not want to show up unprepared and ignorant of the culture. When we are teaching students who do not look like us or have different backgrounds than us, we should approach it with this same effort and zeal. We need to learn as much as we can about their backgrounds so that we can know how to approach them and how to teach them. There are things that are particular to certain cultures that those who are ignorant may view as "bad behavior" when in reality, it is how a child may be based on their cultural norms.

We need to be open to asking people for help, like the man shared in my session, and, in the words of Kendrick Lamar, we need to "be humble".

When I travelled to Finland, I learned how to say hello and thank you in their language. I thought it would be absolutely rude for me to show up and assume that they would speak English. Why do we expect to show up in a classroom full of students of different backgrounds and expect them to speak our language and to conform to our norm when our norm is not their norm? Furthermore, what is normal anyway? Not only do we have to have cross cultural skills when dealing with our students, but we should seek to be cross generational too. Know what young people are in to, learn what they like, and who they like, and use that to reach them. Every time I visit a country, I always attempt to speak their language, and while I don't always pronounce the words right, the locals always appreciate the effort. If you seek to improve your cross-cultural skills, your students will appreciate this too.

Eliminate Cultural Deficit Bias

Cultural deficit bias means that you hold lower expectations for those who have demographics that do not fit the traditional context of society.

Reflections from the Field:

My heart broke today. As an English teacher, it's one of my favorite times of year: National Spelling Bee time! Even students who usually aren't excited about class activities show enthusiasm at the thought of potentially winning their class spelling bee and ultimately representing their class and school on a larger platform. Every day this week when the students had a double period in English class, we held their class spelling bee to determine the winner and runner-up. There are students in each class who are deemed the "smart" kids and who feel they are a shoo-in for this spelling bee gig; the winner was one of the "smart" Black boys. However, this year there were upsets galore and the biggest involved a Black boy who, even after arriving late to school, entered the competition during the second round and wound up being the runner-up! The reaction from the runner-up's classmates was telling, yet expected. They were all shocked. After all, he is not exactly the most studious of the bunch. He learns differently from others and is known best for falling asleep in class and avoiding work by asking for the coveted bathroom pass. It was the reaction of the other teacher in the classroom regarding his runner-up status, however, that reeked of low teacher expectations. The teacher could barely contain her shock about the student coming so close to winning the class spelling bee, which wasn't a delightfully shocked tone. There was just too much surprise in both her tone and facial expression. I was offended and couldn't help but call her out on her implicit-bias-filled reaction by asking her straight-up, "Why exactly ARE you so shocked that he is the spelling bee runner up?". She just stared back at me and shrugged her shoulders while saying, "Well, y'know". "No, I don't know. Enlighten me," was my response. Needless to say, she fell mute. The thought, much less the reality, of this Black boy shattering her dim view of his abilities and actually excelling academically rendered her speechless. Unfortunately, the low teacher expectations that she exhibited today is common in classrooms with Black children across the United States.

What shocked the teacher in my class today welled up tears of joy inside of me. I was so proud of my student. You should've seen the looks on everybody's faces when he spelled word after word correctly! The dropped jaws were literally a sight to behold. I saw my student morph before my very eyes from an unconfident boy who has never done well in school to one of the "cool" kids who earned the respect of his peers. Unfortunately, he also earned the baffled side-eye of one of his teachers. The latter is an experience no student should endure, yet one which Black students — Black male students, especially — endure repeatedly. This phenomenon is not new. As a young girl in the second-grade, I was embarrassed in front of the entire class during a geography game. When it was my turn, the letter was "O" and I said "Ocho Rios", a parish in my parents' homeland of Jamaica where I had just been for weeks earlier that summer. My White teacher, Mrs. Krushell, told me that there was no such place and that if I didn't have an answer, I should just pass my turn instead of wasting time and turning the game into a joke. I went home in tears, told my mom, and thanks to my mom, by the next day, Mrs. Krushell got a detailed lesson on Jamaican geography. She apologized but even at the age of seven,

I knew that even though I was considered to be a "smart" Black girl by my teacher, I still wasn't "that smart". I definitely wasn't smart enough to know something she didn't know, much less to have first-hand experience traveling to this place of which she had never heard. The nerve of me. There needs to be a purposeful paradigm shift in not only what is taught, but how it is taught, and who is teaching it.

- **Vivett Dukes – Teacher, Writer, Advocate, Activist**

NYC/ Long Island, NY

Vivett's story is one we have seen and one some of us have done. Remember the "compliment" 'you speak well' that is reserved for people of color – that is cultural deficit bias, thinking that a Black or Brown student cannot speak properly because of how they look.

Be honest with yourself, have you had moments where you demonstrated cultural deficit bias? Did you assume something about your students without truly giving them the opportunity to show you otherwise? Cultural deficit bias is dangerous, it limits the opportunities we provide to students because we "think" they can't do it. In our mind, we tell ourselves that we will give them an easier assignment so that they can "succeed" knowing all the while we did it because we did not believe they could – there is the ugly Belief gap again.

So what will you do to ensure that you eliminate cultural deficit bias and develop your cultural competency?

_____

_____

_____

Reflections from the Field:

In education, relationships are key. One of the best decisions I made was to teach and live in the same community. The importance of this should not be overlooked. It gives me the opportunity to see my students and their families outside of school, at church, the grocery store, and everywhere else in between. Through this lens, I am constantly reminded that the students I teach are individuals first, and that school is a fraction of the context in which we live. It helps me to maintain and cherish a broad view of my students. I can recall this instance where it was particularly helpful when I had a student once who was being lazy and uncooperative, at times defiant, in class. I tried all I could to encourage him and modify his behavior. I used every tactic I knew, to no avail.

Honestly, I was beginning to think - this kid is a bad person. Then one day, he was my cashier at the grocery store. I was amazed. He was intelligent, helpful and polite, even though he was embarrassed to see me. When I was done, I told him, "Hey, I'm proud of you." The next day in class, I wrote him a letter that basically said, "I always knew you were capable of greatness, and I caught a glimpse of it yesterday at Publix. There is no need to be embarrassed because the skills and talents that you will develop while working there will give you an advantage in your careers as an adult. How do I know? I worked at the grocery store as a teen." Then I went back a few more times, masking my intentions, and making sure to tell him each time, "I am proud of you." Needless to say, his behavior and academic performance in class improved dramatically. And he became an 'A' student and school leader.

In my opinion, discipline should exist for the purpose of behavior modification. And yet, in a myriad of instances, especially at school, we use discipline as a form of punishment. Well, what do we do when the punishment does not achieve the desired result?

I can recall PJ's story. PJ was a student who came to me in the 9th grade. I thought he was an extremely difficult student, and he gave his other teachers double the agony he gave me. My eyes were opened one day when we had a chat. I warned him, "PJ, if you don't stop being unruly and defiant, you're going to get into big trouble." I apologize in advance for his reply, "Mr. Bethel, I don't give a *&%#. I'm not afraid. I've already experience the worst that the system can do to me." Wow! I sat and listened as he poured out his story, which began way back in first grade with punishments for being talkative. His punishment grew from being sent to the corner of the room, to being pulled into the hallway, and all the way to being sent to the principal. In 2nd and 3rd grade, he was still talkative, but his punishment grew to having detention and in-school suspension. In all this time, no one paused long enough to realize that none of this was hindering him from being talkative. By 4th grade, feeling misunderstood and picked on, he grew to talking back, which precipitated his punishment increasing all the way to parent meetings and out of school suspension. He was expelled from his first school in 5th grade for a series of unruly behavior and defiance. He had been expelled two more times before he met me. Once, in 7th grade, after he refused to step out of the classroom, the school deputy took him out in hand-cuffs, and he spent the weekend locked up. My heart ached hearing all this. He was absolutely right, school punishment was no longer any deterrent, and what we had listed as discipline practices had failed to alter his decisions or behavior. And, explained through his voice and his lens, I could agree that none of it was his fault . Just like in academic instruction, when the discipline practices we have in place do not work, it is the responsibility of the professionals (adults) to be creative and persistent until uncovering what does work for the good of each individual child. The same shoe does not fit every foot, and so, the same consequences will not 'turn around every child'.

-   Casey Bethel, 2017 Georgia Teacher of the Year

Restorative Justice

What is the purpose of discipline?

Just as Casey talked about in his passage, he always opens up our collaborative sessions on the School-to-prison pipeline by asking the question above. The answers vary. Some people say to correct, some day to control, and others say to train. I argue that the purpose of discipline should be to teach. Everything we do, every lesson we teach, every word we speak to our students, should serve the purpose of teaching them. Every moment in the school day opens the door for a teachable moment. Discipline should be no different. Many times, behaviors are a symptom of deeper issues that we need to address in order to teach students how to cope with those issues. Restorative justice is a process that seeks to restore a child back to their whole self. The most powerful aspect of restorative justice is that this form of justice not only benefits students who have committed offenses, but it also benefits the school community at large in that we learn how to move forward together.

No one knew how to handle Jamal – as a matter of fact – many people were at a loss for how to handle many of our boys that school year. Before they even arrived, I looked at their data and noticed that many of our incoming students were not performing on grade level, so we knew that we needed to differentiate our approach when it came to this group of students.

Jamal was always angry. Upon first interaction with him, it would be easy to cast him off as another angry black boy, but I knew something else was amiss. His 7th grade teacher made sure to stop by for a visit to let me know how "bad" he was and how glad she was to be rid of him. I am careful not to let others' experiences with students, or people in general, to be my experience. I get to know my students first and then formulate my OWN opinion of them. We need to be cautious of this as educators – let the students have a fair chance and a fresh start – your experience will not be everyone else's.

The Principal came to my room one Friday, and I knew it must have been bad because he rarely made a stop to my room.

"Kelisa, I need you to help me with Jamal," he half pleaded. Jamal had already been suspended several times; the principal believed he simply did not care, and it was only November.

"I'll try, but you have to let me do this the way I want to do it" I committed to him.

I sat Jamal down and just asked him what was going on. He refused to talk or even look me in my eyes, so I gave him a pencil and some paper and asked him to write since he was not going to talk.

For many of our sessions he said nothing and wrote nothing, but eventually he started to write: *I miss my dad. Everyone thinks I am bad – I am not good.*

I swallowed a lump when I read that he thought he was not good. What had we done I thought. Jamal had been conditioned to believe he was bad and started to view himself as such. Jamal's father was deployed to Afghanistan, and he was afraid of losing him.

After I started gaining his trust, I had his mother come in so we could talk through some of the behaviors she was seeing at home, and we were seeing at school. We then formulated a behavior change contract (see below) that we worked on together. He started to eventually become more engaged and involved in our conversations and even articulated his own goals with me. We worked together, and many times, his mother came into the conversations as well so that we could talk about how he was doing both at school and at home. I also made sure that everyone who had a need to know the plan knew it, especially the other teachers in the building so that they could encourage him to be able to stick with his plan. We also ensured that we got him counseling to learn how to channel his feelings about his father being gone.

Sample Behavior Change Contract

(1) I _____ agree to _____
(name)   (specify behavior you want to change)

_____

(2) I will begin on _____ and plan to reach my goal of _____
(start date)   (specify final goal)

_____

by _____.
(final target date)

(3) In order to reach my final goal, I have devised the following schedule of minigoals. For each step in my program, I will give myself the reward listed.

(minigoal 1)	(target date)	(reward)
(minigoal 2)	(target date)	(reward)
(minigoal 3)	(target date)	(reward)

My overall reward for reaching my final goal will be _____

(4) I have gathered and analyzed data on my target behavior and have identified the following strategies for changing my behavior: _____

_____

(5) I will use the following tools to monitor my progress toward reaching my final goal:

_____
(list any charts, graphs, or journals you plan to use)

I sign this contract as an indication of my personal commitment to reach my goal.

_____   _____
(your signature)   (date)

I have recruited a helper who will witness my contract and _____

_____
(list any way in which your helper will participate in your program)

_____   _____
(witness's signature)   (date)

The purpose of working with Jamal was to restore him, to heal him, and to repair him so that he could be reintegrated.

These are the pillars of restorative justice: identification of the issue, repairing the issue, and rebuilding. Jamal went from a "problem" student to a student who could handle his problems, identify his problems, and view his problems as an opportunity for growth. My principal saw how successful this was and asked that we do it for all students struggling on our grade level. We saw a reduction in disciplinary issues by 60% after we implemented restorative justice as an intervention. The idea of a Behavior Contract allowed the students who needed it to see their short term wins and to learn how to celebrate the small successes.

Afterword: Possibilities Met, Promises Kept

We are at a critical point in this country for our youth. Times are harder now than they have ever been for our children. They are facing pressures that we never had to face during our adolescence, but unfortunately, as new challenges have presented themselves, old challenges have remained and even worsened. We must provide our students with multiple pathways to success. We must change our implicit and explicit biases that have contributed to the school-to-prison pipeline, and we must acknowledge that the problem actually exists. It is easy to turn a blind eye when you are teaching in a de facto segregated school and this is not something that you are seeing, but 67% of students across this nation are feeling the impact of this epidemic. Our children are at risk and we must act now! So how do we ensure that we give them possibilities that allow them to be a person that has the potential to become whoever they desire to be, and how can we promise, declare, and assure that we will do this:

1. **Join the School to Prison Pipeline Consortium**

   Founded by two veteran educators and athletic coaches with a passion for equity issues, DRIVE Educational System is uniting a coalition of individuals, organizations, and institutions around the, "Most critical civil rights issue of our time" the Pipeline to Prison (Arne Duncan, 2014). DRIVE offers a series of Professional Development workshops to address discipline dis-proportionality across school systems nationwide. Partnering directly with administration and staff, the DRIVE team works fervently in the trenches to first build a culture of TRUST, belonging and self-reflection. This creates a foundation for meaningful action and builds a climate where we can shed light on and uncover the implicit bias that exists within all individuals and institutions. Utilizing their framework, based on scientifically backed research, to attack this critical issue from a multitude of fronts (interpersonally, culturally and structurally) the DRIVE team continues to search for partners to build a coalition to dismantle the School-to-Prison Pipeline. For more information on how you can become part of the solution and join this consortium, please visit:

<http://www.thedriverevolution.com/>

2. **Close the Belief Gap** – Believe in students' abilities and believe in them enough to realize that we have to change in order to help them realize their potential. Believe in them enough to invest time in them to get to know them beyond the exterior. Believe in them enough to change your practices. Believe in them enough to care about this issue even if it does not directly impact *your* students or *your* children because these are OUR children – all of them! Believe that they can perform just as well as your students who come from affluence – believe in them!

3. **Raise Awareness** – As I used to say to my Middle Schoolers, we need to get "woke" about this issue. Talk to

as many people about the school-to-prison pipeline as you can. Do research on your own school's discipline policies or your child's discipline policy. Identify whether or not the policy is a part of the problem or lending to the solution. We need to stay woke, remain vigilant, and speak up about the school-to-prison pipeline.

4. **Be the Change** – As Mahatma Gandhi said, we must be the change we want to see in this world. We have to realize that it starts with 'me', it starts with you, and it starts with us. A few years ago, I almost gave up on a student, we will call her "Alexis". Alexis could read on an 11th grade level in the 8th grade, her standardized scores were in the 7th and 8th stanine, but Alexis was failing every subject – Alexis had an issue with apathy not aptitude. We met with Alexis' parents, the counselor, placed her on a Student Support Team, sent her to homework help, but she still continued to fail. I was so frustrated after months of battling to get her to care – I thought to myself, This child does not want to succeed so why should I care because obviously she

137

doesn't. That evening as I was driving home I found myself blaming everyone, her, her parents, her previous teachers – everyone was at fault in my mind, but as I pointed a finger at everyone else, I had four more fingers pointing back at me. I had to truly ask myself: Have YOU done EVERYTHING YOU can do? And my honest answer was no, I can do more – there is more to be done. When Alexis came into the classroom the next day, I was sitting right beside her desk. She looked very confused. As she took her seat, I handed her a list of tasks that she would be completing and I said: WE are doing this TOGETHER – you are not allowed to fail any longer. Alexis said if you believe that I can do this, I will do it. Change did not occur overnight – there were days when I was still frustrated, sitting side-by-side with Alexis, but I never gave up. By meeting Alexis where she was, working with my colleagues, and allowing Alexis to have a voice and a choice in what her educational goals should look like, this child grew in every subject area. What I realized through that experience is that change had to start with me. If there is a problem in my classroom, it starts with me. If a student has a problem, the solution lies within me. If we see something we do not like within our schools, it starts with us making a decision to become change agents. To move from conversation to action, to move from 'I' to 'we' because we are better together, but it starts with us.

I say this story to remind you that in order to make change we have to be the change and live the change. We are the solution to this problem, but we must begin the process by first critically looking at ourselves and then realizing that we cannot accomplish the issues of education for our youth in isolation. It starts with us: parents, students, teachers, administrators and community members, deciding to work in unity because their dreams can only come true when teams follow through. We have to make a decision to say, no more, not on my watch will I allow the school-to-prison pipeline to exist. We have to realize that we are who the youth have been waiting for. We have the power to fix this, and we must fix this because students deserve it. We can and we must dismantle this pipeline – together – we can

end this once and for all and fulfill the promise of

dismantling the pipeline and give our students endless

possibilities!

References

Black, S. (2004). Safe Schools Don't Need Zero Tolerance. *American School Board Journal*, 191(1). 62-64.

Fries, K., & DeMitchell, T. (2007). Zero Tolerance and the Paradox of Fairness: Viewpoints from the Classroom. *Journal of Law & Education*, 36(2). 211-229.

Supreme Court declines to hear zero tolerance case. (2012). Retrieved from <http://www.ocspecialedattorney.com/supreme-court-declines-hear-zero-tolerance-case/>

Vanneman, A., Hamilton, L., Anderson, J., & Rahman, T. (July 2009). Achievement Gaps: How black and white students in public schools perform in mathematics and reading on the National Assessment of Educational Progress. Retrieved from <http://nces.ed.gov/nationsreportcard/pubs/studies/2009455.asp

ABOUT THE AUTHOR

Kelisa Wing is an Assistant Principal in New York.

In 2017, she was selected as a State Teacher of the Year and honored with the Outstanding Alumnae Award from University of Maryland University College. She is a 2016 Association of Supervision Curriculum and Development (ASCD) Emerging Leader. Wing is the founder of Squad Up for Education, Inc., which was birthed through her vision of creating partnerships with parents and community members to ensure that students can be successful.

She writes for Education Post, ASCD In Service, ASCD Express, and is the author of the memoir *Weeds and Seeds: How to Stay Positive in the Midst of Life's Storms*

Kelisa holds a Bachelor's Degree in English from the University of Maryland University College, a Master's Degree in Education and an Educational Specialist Degree in Educational Leadership and Curriculum and Instruction from the University of Phoenix, and is currently working on her Doctoral Degree.

Kelisa lives in New York with her husband and children. You can follow Kelisa on Twitter @kelisa_l2teach.

Made in the USA
Monee, IL
08 October 2021